BIAMS

BIAMS is a membership association of colleges and individuals which brings together people from all parts of the Christian church who are involved in the study of mission. It exists:

- To promote the study of the history, theology and practice of mission.
- To encourage awareness of major issues in contemporary mission.
- To provide a meeting point for mutual enrichment, challenge and collaboration in mission. For more information visit www.biams.org.uk.

Global Mission Network

The Global Mission Network of CTBI was set up as an ecumenical space in which experience and perspectives on mission could be shared in order to benefit Churches and agencies in their mission work. GMN has now been superseded by The Churches Network for Mission, which seeks to assist the churches, agencies and the ecumenical bodies of the Four Nations in the common task of participating in God's mission in the world. See www.ctbi.org.uk/CA/13.

Global Connections

Global Connections (GC) is a network of over 300 UK based mission agencies, churches, colleges and support services linked together for resources, learning and representation. The network aims to serve, equip and develop churches in order to fulfil the shared vision of 'mission at the heart of the church, the church at the heart of mission'. GC was formerly known as the Evangelical Missionary Alliance and has its roots in bringing together evangelical mission agencies. For more information visit www.globalconnections.co.uk.

John Clark served in Christian literature work and publishing for eleven years until the 1979 Islamic Revolution. For the next seven years he was Regional Secretary for the Middle East and Pakistan for the Church Mission Society travelling widely in the region, followed by five years as Head of CMS' Communications Division. In 1992 he became Secretary of the Church of England's Partnership for World Mission (PWM) which linked the Church of England world mission agencies with its Synodical structures. In 2000 he was appointed Secretary of the Church of England's Board of Mission, which in 2003 was restructured with the Board for Social Responsibility, Hospital Chaplaincy Council and Committee for Minority Ethnic Concerns into the Church of England's Mission and Public Affairs Division of which he became the first Director, retiring in April 2007. Among other roles he has been a member of successive Mission Commissions of the Anglican Communion and in retirement is involved with a number of charities involved in Christian presence and witness in the Middle East.

Philip Knights is a Catholic priest of the Diocese of Westminster. He is currently Priest Administrator of Marychurch, Hatfield and Diocesan Director of *Missio*. He also sits upon the *Overseas Mission Committee* of the Catholic Bishops Conference of England and Wales. Before his current posts he taught at the Missionary Institute London and was a member of the *Catholic Missionary Society* and its successor body *CASE (The Catholic Agency to Support Evangelisation)*. He is also at present the Executive Secretary of the *British and Irish Association of Mission Studies* (BIAMS), one of the collaborating networks in this research. His interests in mission have traversed Central and Southern Africa and the UK. His doctoral thesis concerned models of mission tested against groups in Southern Africa and how in distinct ways they sought to be authentically African. He conducted research on behalf of the Catholic Bishops Conference on *Evangelisation in England and Wales*. He has also published analysis of and reports from various significant initiatives in Catholic evangelisation as *Changing Evangelisation*, which was part of the *Churches Together in Britain and Ireland*, 'Changing Mission' series. More recently he has been engaged in issues of environmental justice and the theology of mission.

Martin Lee has a 1st Class degree in Physics with Maths and initially started his career as a secondary school teacher. He then worked for 25 years as Director of a Christian Relief and Development agency, specialising in refugees and children caught in conflict situations, spending long periods in SE Asia and East Africa. Martin now serves

as Director of Global Connections, a UK mission network comprising of the majority of evangelical mission agencies and a growing number of churches. He also serves on various mission and charity trustee bodies. Martin is also actively involved in the European Evangelical Mission Association and the WEA Mission Commission. He specialises in researching and understanding mission trends. His passion is to see churches in the UK engaging in mission both locally and globally. He is concerned that such mission is relevant to the 21st Century with an emphasis on learning from the majority world and integral in approach. He is married to Georgina, who teaches English to refugees and the longer term settled community in Coventry. They are passionate about trade justice and own a small fair-trade business. Martin and Georgina have two daughters, a son and one grand-daughter and are active members in a local independent evangelical church.

Janice Price is World Mission Policy Adviser for the Archbishops' Council of the Church of England. Previously she was Executive Secretary of the Churches Together in Britain and Ireland Global Mission Network and Director of Development and Training in the Anglican Diocese of Worcester. She is a Lay Reader (Licensed Minister) in the Church of England and has served in local churches in urban, suburban and rural parishes. Holding two research based degrees from King's College London her current research interests are in the use and potential of Qualitative Research software in mission research and the development of partnership in Anglican world church relationships. She is an Honorary Lay Canon of Worcester Cathedral. Publications include *Telling Our Faith Story* (1999 and reprinted 2009), Grove Books and *Equipping Your Church in a Spiritual Age*, Church House Publishing, 2005. She is one of the two Co-convenors of the Foundations for Mission Study Theme for the Edinburgh 2010 World Mission Conference.

Anne Richards is National Adviser: mission theology, new religious movements and alternative spiritualities for the Archbishops' Council of the Church of England. She is the convener of the ecumenical Mission Theology Advisory Group which produces practical mission resources on gospel and culture issues, including *The Search for Faith and the Witness of the Church* (1996), *Presence and Prophecy* (2002), *Transparencies* (2002) and the beautifully illustrated *Sense Making Faith* (2007), a resource book for Christians who are interested in sharing their faith with others outside the Church. Dr Richards also maintains a website www.spiritualjourneys.org.uk based on *Sense Making Faith* for Christians and other spiritual seekers. She has contributed to many books on mission-related subjects, and written numerous articles on mission issues, theology and contemporary spirituality.

Paul Rolph spent ten years as a science teacher and thirty years as a teacher educator ending his full-time career as head of a faculty of teacher education in a Church of England university college. Paul retired from full-time work in 1998. He took up part-time employment as a county ecumenical officer and as a university postgraduate supervisor of ministers of religion who are researching for a higher degree in pastoral

and empirical theology. Paul has a particular interest in drawing on his scientific background to develop empirical methods in the study of church and educational institutions. He researches relationships between well-being and spirituality and how they are, and might be, fostered by educational and religious institutions. Paul is currently a research fellow in theology. He is married to Jenny, a social psychologist, who has many years of teaching experience in higher education. They publish research papers jointly. Jenny and Paul have three married daughters and one married son and twelve grandchildren.

Nigel Rooms is Director of Ministry and Mission in the Anglican Diocese of Southwell and Nottingham, Associate Priest at Bestwood Park with Rise Park LEP and honorary Canon of Christchurch Cathedral in the Diocese of Mt. Kilimanjaro, Tanzania. He worked as Mission Partner in Tanzania for seven years in the 1990's developing an innovative Theological Education by Extension Course in Swahili, running an International congregation and building a new Church. He holds a Th.D in Missiology from Birmingham University (U.K.) and has research and other interests in contextual theology (particularly in England), adult theological education, leadership and ministerial formation and emerging church as well as theological foundations for mission. He is married to Karen, also a priest, and they have two teenage sons. They live in inner-city Nottingham where enjoys working on his allotment.

Anderson, A., (2004) *An Introduction to Pentecostalism* (Cambridge: Cambridge University Press)

Anderson, A., (2007) *Spreading Fires: The Missionary Nature of Early Pentecostalism* (London: SCM)

Anglican Consultative Council, (1984) *Bonds of Affection*, Report of the Sixth meeting (Anglican Communion Office)

Batty, D., and Campbell, E., (2008) 'Teen Challenge: 50 Years of Miracles', *Assemblies of God Heritage* 28

Bevans, S., Schroeder., R., (2004) *Constants in Context: a theology of mission for today* (Maryknoll: Orbis)

Board of Mission, (1994) *Breaking New Ground* (London: Church House Publishing)

Boff, C., and Boff, L., (1987) *Introducing Liberation Theology* (Maryknoll: Orbis)

Bosch, D., (1991) *Transforming Mission* (Maryknoll: Orbis Books)

Brookes, A., *The Alpha Phenomenon*, (London: CTBI publishing)

Buhlmann, W., (1977) *The Coming of the Third Church* (Maryknoll:Orbis)

Burgess, S., and van der Maas, E., (eds.), (2002) *New International Dictionary of Pentecostal and Charismatic Movements* (Grand Rapids, MI: Zondervan)

Donovan, V., (1978) *Christianity Rediscovered* (SCM: London)

Donovan, V., (1989) *The Church in the Midst of Creation* (Maryknoll: Orbis)

Doyle, D., (2004) *Communion Ecclesiology* (Maryknoll: Orbis)

Finney, J., (1992) *Finding Faith Today* (Swindon: Bible Society)

Francis, L., and Robbins, M., (2006) *Urban Hope and Spiritual Health: The Adolescent Voice* (London: Epworth Press)

Guttierez, G., (1973) *A Theology of Liberation* (London: SCM)

Hayes. M., (ed) (2006)*New Religious movements in the Catholic Church* (London: Continuum Publications)

Hammond, J.L. and B. (1918) *The Town Labourer, 1760-1832* (London: Longmans Green)

Hodges, M., (1963)*The Indigenous Church* (Springfield, MO: Gospel Publishing House)

Hoggard, L., (2005) *How to be Happy* (London: BBC Books)

Hollenweger, W., *Pentecostalism: Origins and Developments Worldwide* (Peabody, MA: Hendrickson, 1997)

Inter-Anglican Commission on Mission and Evangelism (2006) *Communion in Mission*, (Anglican Communion Office)

Kahneman D., Krueger A.B., Schkade D., et al. (2006). 'Would you be happier if you were richer? A focusing illusion'. *Science, 312,* 1908-1910. (Article available at www.sciencemag.org/cgi/content/abstract/312/5782/1908)

Kaye, B., (2008) *An Introduction to World Anglicanism* (Cambridge: Cambridge University Press)

Kim, S., (1987), 'Is "Minjung Theology" a Christian Theology?', *Calvin Theological Journal* 22:2

Kim, S., (2007) 'The Problem of Poverty in Post-War Korean Christianity: *Kibock Sinang* or *Minjung* Theology?', *Transformation* 24:1 (Jan 2007) 43-50.

Knights, P., (ed.) (2007) *Changing Evangelisation* (London: CTBI)

Lambeth Conference (1998)*The Virginia Report, online at* www.lambethconference. org/1998/documents/report-1.pdf

Layard, R., (2005) *Happiness: Lessons from a new science* (London: Allen Lane)

Lee, Y-H., (2009)*The Holy Spirit Movement in Korea* (Oxford: Regnum Books)

Libānio, J. B., (1993) 'Hope, Utopia, Resurrection' in Ellacuría., I and Sobrino J., (eds) *Mysterium Liberationis* (Maryknoll: Orbis)

Lyubomirsky, S., K M Sheldon,& D Schkade (2005) 'Pursuing Happiness: The Architecture of Sustainable Change,' Review of General Psychology, Special Issue: Positive Psychology 9 (20: 111-131)

Ma, W., and Ma, J., (2010) *Mission in the Spirit: Towards a Pentecostal-Charismatic Missiology* (Oxford: Regnum Books)

Ma, W., (2008) 'David Yonggi Cho's Theology of Blessing: A new theological base and direction', in Young San Theological Institute (ed.), *Dr. Yonggi Cho's Ministry and Theology: A Commemorative Collection for the 50th Anniversary of Dr. Yonggi Cho's Ministry*, 2 vols. (Gunpo, Korea: Hansei University Logos), I:179-200.

Ma, W., (2007) "When the Poor Are Fired Up": The Role of Pneumatology in Pentecostal-Charismatic Mission', *Transformation* 24:1

Ma, W., (2005) 'Full Circle Mission: A Possibility of Pentecostal Missiology, *Asian Journal of Pentecostal Studies* 8:1

Ma, W., (2006) 'Pentecostal Eschatology: What Happened When the Wave Hit the West End of the Ocean', Hunter, H., and Robeck, C., Jr. (eds.), *The Azusa Street Revival and Its Legacy* (Cleveland, TN: Pathway)

Macchia, F., (2006) *Baptized in the Spirit: A Global Pentecostal Theology* (Grand Rapids: Zondervan)

McPartlan, P., (1995) *Sacrament of Salvation*(Edinburgh: T & T Clark)

Marks, L., (1992) 'The Hallelujah Lasses: Working Class Women in the Salvation Army in English Canada 1882-92' in *Gender Conflicts* Eds. Franca Iacovetta and Mariana Valverde (Toronto: University of Toronto Press)

Martin, D., (1990) *Tongues of Fire: The Explosion of Protestantism in Latin America* (Oxford: Blackwell)

Martin, R., and Williamson P., (eds.) (1995) *Pope John Paul II and the New Evangelisation* (San Francisco: Ignatius Press)

Mellor, H., Yates, T., (ed.) (2004) *Mission, Violence and Reconciliation* (Calver: Cliff College)

Menzies, R., (2004) *Empowered for Witness: The Spirit in Luke-Acts* (London: T & T Clark)

Milbank, J., (1990) *Theology* and *Social Theory* (Oxford: Blackwell)

Miller, D., and Yamamori, T., (2007) *Global Pentecostalism: The New Face of Christian Social Engagement* (Berkley: University of California Press)

Mission Theological Advisory Group, (1996) *The Search for Faith and the Witness of the Church* (London: Church House Publishing)

Mission Theological Advisory Group, (2002) *Presence and Prophecy* (London: Church House Publishing)

Mission Theological Advisory Group (2002) *Transparencies: Pictures of Mission through Prayer and Reflection* (London: Church House Publishing)

Mission and Public Affairs Division, (2004) *Mission-Shaped Church* (London: Church House Publishing)

Moltmann, J., (1977) The Church in the Power of the Spirit: A Contribution to Messianic Ecclesiology (London: SCM)

Newbigin, L., *The Gospel in a Pluralist Society,* (London: SPCK)

Nichols, A., (1991) *The Shape of Catholic Theology* (Collegeville: Liturgical Press)

O'Meara, T., (2007) *God in the World: A Guide to Karl Rahner's Theology*, (Liturgical Press: Collegeville)

Oswald, N., and Pawdthavee, N., (2005) 'Does Happiness Adapt? A Longitudinal Study of Disability with Implications for Economists and Judges' (Mimeo; University of Warwick)

Petrella, I., (2008)*Beyond Liberation Theology: A Polemic* (London: SCM Press)

Pope Paul VI *Evangelii Nuntiandi*

Ratzinger, R., (1987) *Principles of Catholic Theology: Building Stones for a Fundamental Theology* (San Francisco: Ignatius Press)

Rendle, G., Mann, A., (2003) *Holy Conversations: strategic planning as a spiritual practice for congregations*, (Herndan, VA: Alban Institute)

The Rite of Christian Initiation of Adults: A Study Book, (1988) (St Thomas More Centre: London)

Schreiter, R., (1996) *Reconciliation: Mission and Ministry in a Changing Social Order,* (Maryknoll: Orbis Books)

Sider, R., and Unruch, H., (2005) *Saving Souls, Serving Society* (Oxford: Oxford University Press)

Synan, V., (2000) 'A Healer in the House? A Historical Perspective on Healing in the Pentecostal/Charismatic Tradition' *Asian Journal of Pentecostal Studies* 3:2

Stronstad, R., (1984) *The Charismatic Theology of St. Luke* (Peabody, MA: Hendrickson)

Suh, N-D., (1983) 'Toward a Theology of Han', in Kim, Y., (ed.), *Minjung Theology: People as the Subjects of History* (Maryknoll, NY: Orbis Books)

Taylor, J., (1998)*The Uncancelled Mandate* (London: Church House Publishing)

TEAC., (2008) *Towards an Anglican Understanding of Mission and Evangelism,* Signposts No 2, (Anglican Communion Office)

Tillard J-M., (1992) *Church of Churches the ecclesiology of Communion* (Collegeville: Liturgical Press)

Tillich, P., (1978) *Systematic Theology I* (London: SCM Press)

USPG Anglicans in World Mission, (2008) *Our Theological Basis and Ways of Working*

Von Hügel Institute and the Margaret Beaufort Institute of Theology, (2006) *Going Forth: An Enquiry into Evangelisation and Renewal in the Roman Catholic Church in England and Wales* (Cambridge)

Warren, R., (1995) *Building Missionary Congregations* (London: Church House Publishing)

www.biams.org.uk

www.caseresources.org/evangelisation/evangelisation_newevangelisation.htm

www.edinburgh2010.org/en/about-edinburgh-2010.html

www.globalconnections.co.uk

www.martynmission.cam.ac.uk/pages/hmc-seminar-papers.php

www.oikoumene.org/en/resources/documents/assembly/porto-alegre-2006/3-preparatory-and-background-documents/final-report-of-the-special-commission-on-orthodox-participation-in-the-wcc.html

www.oikoumene.org/en/resources/documents/wcc-commissions/mission-and-evangelism/cwme-world-conference-athens-2005.html

www.rcia.org.uk/Resources/Books.html

www.religionandsocialpolicy.org

www.surveymonkey.com

Yates, T., (1996) *Christian Mission in the Twentieth Century* (Cambridge: Cambridge University Press)

Yung, H., (2004) 'The Missiological Challenge of David Yonggi Cho's Theology', in Ma, W., Menzies, W., and Bae, H-S (eds.), *David Yonggi Cho: A Close Look at His Theology and Ministry* (Baguio, Philippines: APTS Press)

Foundations for Mission

'Mission' seems to be on everyone's lips these days. It's a feel-good word, suggesting purpose, direction and transformative change. Christians talk about mission a great deal and it seems to be integral to every dynamic church agenda. But what does all this mission talk have to do with God and with what Christians actually do?

This book is the result of research conducted to answer these questions. Set up in response to the Foundations for Mission study theme of the 2010 Edinburgh World Mission Conference, *Foundations for Mission* shows how the relationship of language, theology and praxis in the UK and Ireland is a complicated and messy affair. Using website analysis, a theological survey and in-depth interviews, the research group asked leaders of churches, agencies and other mission bodies to examine their underlying drivers and purpose for mission. A picture emerges of profound commitment to hospitality, openness, and reconciliation from the Christian community, and the offering of God's love for all, but *how* that happens, and *who* exactly should be involved in the process is much less clear.

Foundations for Mission offers insights to all interested in the theology and practice of mission and contains full data analysis for the serious researcher. It also contains useful tools for continuing mission audit and reflection.

churches together

IN BRITAIN AND IRELAND©

ISBN 978-0-85169-363-7

9 780851 693637

Front cover photo: shutterstock©Leigh Prather
Back cover photo: shutterstock©Neale Cousland